WORLD BELIEFS AND CULTURES

Christianity

Revised and Updated

Sue Penney

Heinemann Library
Chicago, Illinois

Customer Service 888-454-2279
Visit our website at www.heinemannraintree.com

Designed by Steve Mead and Debbie Oatley
Printed and bound in China by Leo Paper Group

12 11 10 09 08
10 9 8 7 6 5 4 3 2 1

New edition ISBNs: 1-4329-0313-6 (hardcover)
                       1-4329-0320-9 (hardcover)
13-digit ISBNs: 978-1-4329-0313-8 (hardcover)
                    978-1-4329-0320-6 (paperback)

The Library of Congress has cataloged the first edition as follows:
Penney, Sue.
    Christianity / Sue Penney.
        p. cm. -- (World beliefs and cultures)
    Includes bibliographical references and index.
    ISBN 1-57572-355-7 (library binding)
    1. Christianity--Juvenile literature. [1. Christianity.] I. Title. II. Series.

BR125.5 .P46 2000
230--dc21
                            00-029590

Acknowledgments
The publishers would like to thank the following for permission to reproduce copyright material: Quotations from the Bible are taken from *The Good News Bible*, published by the Bible Society/Harper Collins Publishers Ltd, UK © American Bible Society, 1966, 1971, 1976, 1992. Page 19: "Open Our Eyes, Lord" © Maranatha! Music, administered by Copycare, PO Box 77, Halisham, BN21 3EF.

The publishers would like to thank the following for permission to reproduce photographs: Alamy pp. 13, 39 (Aliki Image Library/Aliki Sapountzi); Ancient Art & Architecture p. 8; C.M. Dixon p. 9; Andes Press Agency/Carlos Reyes-Manzo pp. 4, 5, 7, 12, 19, 20, 25, 28, 30, 32, 33, 34, 40; Art Directors/ Helene Rogers p. 37; Circa Photo Library pp. 36, 31; Corbis pp. 18 (Ariel Skelley), 21, 35 (Owen Franken); e.t. Archive p. 10; Format p. 42; Giraudon/Bridgeman p. 17; Hutchison Library pp. 23 (Nigel Howard), 27 (B. Regent); J. Allan Cash Ltd. pp. 14, 22, 38, 43; Mary Evans Picture Library p. 11; Sonia Halliday Photographs p. 16; The Bridgeman Art Library pp. 6, 15, 41; The Stock Market pp. 24, 26; TIPS Images/Angelo Cavalli p. 29. Background image on cover and inside book from istockphoto.com/Bart Broek.

Cover photo of a statue showing Veronica offering a cloth to Jesus reproduced with permission of © PhotoEdit Inc./Robert W. Ginn.

The publishers would like to thank Dennis Martin for his comments in the preparation of this book.

Every effort has been made to contact copyright holders of any material reproduced in this book. Any

Contents

Some words are shown in bold, **like this**. You can find out what they mean by looking in the glossary.

Dates: In this book, dates are followed by the letters BCE (Before the Common Era) or CE (Common Era). This is instead of using BC (Before Christ) and AD (*Anno Domini,* meaning "in the year of our Lord"). The date numbers are the same in both systems.

Introducing Christianity

Christianity is the most widely held religious belief in the world. Christians can be divided into three main groups. **Orthodox** Christians live mainly in eastern countries, especially around Greece and the former Soviet Union. In other parts of the world (Europe, the Americas, Australia, and Africa, for example) most Christians follow the **Roman Catholic** or **Protestant** traditions. Within these main groups, there are hundreds of smaller groups. Some have millions of members, while others have only a few. Not all the groups and individuals share exactly the same teachings, but they do all share the most important beliefs.

What do Christians believe?

Christians believe that there is one God, revealed in three "persons"—God the Father, God the Son, and God the Holy Spirit. This belief in one God in three persons is called the **Trinity**. Even Christians agree that it is a complicated idea, but it is the basis of Christian teaching about God. It may help you to think of other things that are the same but different—for example, water, steam, and ice.

Christians teach that God the Father is a spirit who is **eternal** and the creator of the universe. He is a loving father who cares about what he made. In recent years, some Christians have begun to talk about God as a mother figure as well as a father figure. Christians believe that the most complete demonstration of what God is like was in the man named Jesus, whom they call God the Son.

*A **congregation** gathers outside a church in South Africa.*

Christians believe that Jesus was a man who lived in Palestine—the country now called Israel—2,000 years ago. Christians often call him Jesus **Christ**, which is where the name "Christian" comes from. "Christ" is often used as if it is part of Jesus' name, but it is actually a special title. It comes from the Greek word "Christos." This in turn is a translation of the **Hebrew** word "**Messiah**," which means "someone who is anointed or chosen by God." Hebrew is the language of the **Jews**, and Jesus was a Jew. At the time Jesus was living in Palestine, Jews were waiting for God to send a Messiah. They believed that the Messiah would begin a special kingdom of God on Earth. Christians believe that Jesus was the Messiah.

Christians also believe that Jesus was both completely God and completely man. They believe that he had a special relationship with God the Father, and that, through Jesus' life and teachings, they can see what God is like.

The death of Jesus is especially important for Christians. They believe that he died a horrible death when he was nailed to a cross, but that two days later God the Father brought him back to life. This is called the **resurrection**. For Christians, the resurrection shows that death is not the end. They say that the death and resurrection of Jesus changed the relationship between God and human beings forever, and it is possible for **sins** to be forgiven. "Sin" is a word that describes all wrongdoing that puts up barriers between people and God. Forgiveness of sins is an important part of Christian teaching. Christians believe that Jesus saved them from the results of their sins, which would prevent them from getting close to God. This is the reason why they often call Jesus their Savior.

Christians believe that the Holy Spirit is the power of God that is working in the world today. It cannot be seen, but they believe that they can see its effect in their lives and in the lives of other people. They believe that it is this power that makes it possible to worship God. The Holy Spirit also gives them the power to live their lives in the way that God wants.

Jesus died on a cross, so a cross is an important symbol for Christians.

Christianity fact check

◆ Christianity began in the 1st century CE.

◆ Christians follow the teachings of a man named Jesus, whom they call Christ.

◆ Christians worship in buildings called churches and **cathedrals**.

◆ The Christian holy book is called the **Bible**.

◆ The two symbols used for Christianity are a cross and a fish.
    Jesus died on a cross. The letters of the Greek word for fish spell the initial letters of the Greek words for "Jesus Christ, God's son, Savior"—the most important Christian beliefs.

◆ There are about 1.9 billion Christians worldwide. Christianity is the major religion in the Americas, Europe, and Australia.

Jesus of Nazareth

You can find the places mentioned in this book on the map on page 44.

*This is an **icon**—a sacred painting—of Jesus from an Orthodox church.*

There is very little doubt that the man called Jesus lived in the 1st century CE in Palestine. He is mentioned as a historical figure by the Roman historian Tacitus, who was writing around 115 CE. There are also other Roman writings that mention him, though they are less reliable. However, most of what we know about Jesus comes from the Gospels—the four books of the Bible that are about Jesus' life and work. This account of Jesus' life is taken from what is written in the Gospels.

Jesus' birth

Jesus was not an ordinary baby. His mother, Mary, was a simple peasant girl. Before she was married, she had been told by an **angel** that she would have a baby who would be the Son of God. She was told to call him Jesus. Although Mary was pregnant, Joseph took Mary as his wife. They lived in Nazareth, but at the time when the baby was due to be born, they had to travel to Bethlehem, where Joseph's family came from, because of a **census**. Accommodation was in short supply. When the baby was born, he was placed in an animals' feeding trough. This may have been in a stable, as many people believe. However, animals and people lived much more closely in those days, and it may just mean that Jesus was born in a very poor household. Shepherds looking after their sheep in the fields outside the town were told by angels of the baby's birth. **Wise men** came to visit Jesus, too, but this must have happened later, after a journey that took many months to complete. The Bible says the wise men "came to the house where the young child was."

Early life

Nothing is known about Jesus' early life, except that he visited Jerusalem when he was 12 years old. When he became separated from his parents, they found him in the **Temple**, the most important building in the Jewish religion. He was discussing religious matters with the leaders of Judaism in the Temple, and they were amazed at his understanding.

Titles for Jesus

The men who wrote the Gospels used many different titles for Jesus. "Jesus" is a form of the common Hebrew name Joshua, which means "The Lord saves." "Christ" is the Greek translation of the Hebrew word "Messiah," meaning "anointed one." "The Lord," used by the **disciples** after the resurrection, is the same Greek word that is used for "God."

"Son of Man" is only used by Jesus about himself. It comes from the book of Daniel and describes a character who was given power by God over the world (chapter 7). "Son of God" is used by Jesus himself and by others to show that he shared God's nature. "Son of David" is used because Jewish teaching says that the Messiah would be a descendant of King David, which the Bible says Jesus was.

Most of the Gospels are about Jesus' adult life. He spent about three years preaching, healing people, and teaching in Galilee and in other parts of Palestine. He became popular with many people, some of whom believed that he was the Messiah—the one whom God had chosen. Some followers hoped that he would lead a rebellion against the Romans, who ruled Palestine. This frightened the Jewish leaders, who depended on the Romans for their power. They were also worried that Jesus claimed to forgive sins—a power that was thought to belong to God alone. They saw Jesus as a threat who must be removed.

Death of Jesus

Jesus was accused of **blasphemy**—that is, speaking against God. In Jewish law, this was a crime punished by death. Under Roman rule, the Jews could not execute anyone, so they persuaded the Roman leader that Jesus was a threat to law and order. Jesus was executed by **crucifixion**—being nailed to a cross. Two days later, followers visiting the tomb where he had been buried found it empty. They came to believe that Jesus was alive again. During the next six weeks, they saw him frequently, before he "ascended into heaven." Christians call this event the **ascension**. Whatever happened, they knew that they were not going to see him again. Christians believe that Jesus is still alive, though not in a human body.

The Bible says that Jesus "ascended into heaven," as shown in this modern stained-glass window.

The History of Christianity

Six weeks after the ascension, the disciples were together in a room. They were probably hiding, worried they were going to be killed for being followers of Jesus. The Bible says they heard a noise like a rushing wind and saw what looked like flames resting on each others' heads. It says they were "filled with the Holy Spirit." This event is called **Pentecost**. It changed the disciples completely. They rushed outside and began to preach, telling the crowd what they believed about Jesus.

As time went on, more and more people became interested in what the disciples were teaching. When all the followers were Jews, there were no problems in living as Jews and keeping the Jewish laws. But then people who were not Jews wanted to become followers. This began to cause problems because, at that time, Jews did not mix with gentiles (non-Jews).

Peter's vision

The answer to the problem came in a **vision** to Peter, one of the leaders of the early Christians. In those days, people believed that visions were messages from God. Peter saw a huge piece of cloth being let down from the sky, full of animals, reptiles, and birds. A voice told him to kill and eat them. Peter was horrified, because it was forbidden for Jews to eat most of these animals. The voice told him that God had made everything in the sheet, and it was not for Peter to say what was fit to eat or not. This happened three times.

Soon afterward, Peter received a message from a Roman soldier named Cornelius. Although Cornelius was a gentile, he was very interested in the Jewish religion. The messengers said that Cornelius had been told in a vision to talk to Peter. Peter realized that the two visions were connected. Just as the voice had told him that it was not for him to judge which of the animals he could eat, so it was not for him to judge

This mosaic from Greece shows St. Peter.

who could be told about Jesus Christ. Peter went with the messengers to Cornelius's house and preached to him and his family about Jesus. The Bible says that while Peter was speaking, "the Holy Spirit came down on all those who were listening." This convinced Peter that he was right to preach to non-Jews.

The Council of Jerusalem

From this time on, Peter became convinced that it was right for non-Jews to be told the "Gospel"—the message of Jesus Christ. There were still many Christians who did not agree. To try to sort out the disagreement, a meeting of all the Christian leaders was held in Jerusalem. This meeting was called the Council of Jerusalem. The leaders listened to the evidence from people who had worked among non-Jews, and they agreed that it was God's will that non-Jews should become Christians. Some basic rules were made for everyone to keep. It was agreed that as long as they kept these rules, non-Jews could become Christians without becoming Jews. This was a turning point in the history of Christianity. It meant that non-Jews were accepted as equal Christians. Christianity was free to reach outside Judaism for the first time.

Paul preached at this Roman amphitheater at Ephesus, in modern-day Turkey.

St. Paul

St. Paul was one of the most important preachers in the first century of the Church. He was born in Tarsus, in what is today called Turkey, and was given the name of Saul. He was a dedicated and rather extreme Jew who at first persecuted and killed Christians for what he saw as their blasphemy. He began to persecute Christians in Jerusalem and then gained permission from the Jewish leaders to go to Damascus to hunt out Christians who had escaped there. As he was traveling to Damascus, he had a vision and was converted to Christianity. Once he had persuaded the Christians that his conversion was genuine, he changed his name to Paul—the Roman form of Saul—and spent the rest of his life traveling all over the Roman Empire. He preached mainly to non-Jews and, because of his preaching, Christian communities grew up in many different places. Between visits to them, Paul wrote many letters to his friends in the communities. These were collected and included in the Bible. Christians treasure them for the advice and insights into Christian beliefs that they contain. They believe that Paul's advice is valuable to all Christians, no matter where or when they live.

The growth of Christianity

For the first 200 years of Christianity, Christians were persecuted by the Romans. The Romans did not tolerate religions that forbade worship of the emperor and demanded obedience to God and not Rome. Christianity did both. Christians were tortured and killed in some of the most gruesome ways ever invented. Christians became known for their bravery and their willingness to die for what they believed. Instead of stamping out the new religion, more and more people became Christians.

In 313 CE, Constantine was fighting to become the Roman emperor. He had a vision in which he was promised victory in battle if he painted a Christian symbol on his soldiers' shields. He did so and won the battle. He was so impressed by this that he made Christianity a legal religion and, within 100 years, Christianity had become the official religion of the Roman Empire.

The Church divides

As Christianity developed, its beliefs became more organized. **Creeds** were developed. Difficult questions—such as exactly how Jesus was God and whether he had always been God or had become God—needed answers. As beliefs became more fixed, people began to disagree about them. They were discussing matters that they believed were very important. They affected not only this life, but also life after death. Gradually, it became clear that two groups of opinions were forming. One group was based in Constantinople. The other was based in Rome.

An 11th-century painting shows Constantine and his mother, St. Helena.

Disagreements between the two groups led to heated arguments. In 1054 two letters were exchanged. In the first, the leader in Constantinople refused to accept the authority of the **pope** in Rome. In his reply, the pope declared that the Constantinople group was no longer part of Christianity. The Church split into two groups. The western group, based in Rome under the leadership of a pope, became the Roman Catholic Church. The eastern group, based in Constantinople under the leadership of **patriarchs**, became the Orthodox Church. Both groups claimed to be the "true" Church, although each recognized the other as having valid sacraments (special religious ceremonies).

The Protestant Reformation

In the West, the Roman Catholic Church was the only church for about 500 years. It was very powerful. Then, during the 16th century, people began to question things about the way the Church was run. The invention of printing meant that people could read the Bible for themselves and ask questions about what the Church taught. They became more critical, for example, about some popes, who seemed to be more interested in power than in teaching people about being Christians. People were taxed so that churches could be built. People who paid enough money were given a certificate called an indulgence, which said that God had forgiven their sins.

Martin Luther was a monk who lived in Germany in the 16th century and helped set off the beginning of the Protestant Reformation.

Many people, such as German **monk** Martin Luther, felt that things like this were wrong. Luther and others led a "Reformation," in which people began worshiping on their own and developed some beliefs that were different from those of the Roman Catholic Church. Because they "protested" about things they felt were wrong, they became known as Protestants. These groups were able to gain power in some countries, partly because some European governments were eager to break from the power of the Roman Catholic Church. There are now many different Protestant churches.

In the last 500 years, many changes have taken place. Christianity has spread throughout the world, and now there are Christians in almost every country. In the 15th and 16th centuries, explorers of new lands took their religion with them. In the 19th century, Christianity spread even further as Christian **missionaries** went to other countries. They taught people about Christianity and tried to persuade them to become Christians. Today, Christians try to show their beliefs by helping other people.

Thomas Aquinas (1224/25–1274 CE)

Thomas Aquinas was born to a wealthy Italian family in the 13th century. His relatives were powerful members of the Roman Catholic Church, and he was expected to follow in their footsteps. During his studies at European universities, Aquinas decided to become a Dominican monk instead. The Dominicans were a group of Catholics who lived very simple lives dedicated to studying, preaching, and doing charitable work.

Aquinas studied philosophy, especially the writings of the great ancient Greek philosopher Aristotle. He used Aristotle's ideas to prove the validity of Christian beliefs such as God's existence and His creation of the universe. Until then, the beliefs of Christians were often believed to be at odds with such ideas. Aquinas is remembered as a great religious figure and philosopher.

Branches of Christianity

In Orthodox churches, the iconostasis divides the altar from the rest of the church.

The Roman Catholic Church

Around 900 million people—about half of all the Christians in the world—are Roman Catholic. They make up the majority of Christians in many European countries and most countries of South America. They accept the authority of the pope, who is the central figure of the Roman Catholic Church. Roman Catholic **clergy** are called **priests** and **bishops**. Other churches use these titles, too. Only men may become Roman Catholic priests, and they are not allowed to marry because they have devoted their life to the Church.

The most important Roman Catholic service is called Mass. There are different patterns of worship, but the Mass always includes the service called the **Eucharist**. Roman Catholics believe that the bishops and pope were set up by Jesus himself to govern and teach the Church and to help Christians become holy. They believe that **baptism**, the Eucharist, and other sacraments (special religious ceremonies) bring about actual spiritual effects in the lives of the worshipers.

The Orthodox Church

The second largest Christian group is the Orthodox Church. "Orthodox" is a Greek word that means "right praise" or "right worship." Orthodox Christians believe that they continue the teachings of the Church as Jesus began it. Most Orthodox Christians live in eastern Europe and Russia, but there are many thousands of Orthodox Christians living in the United States, Europe, and Australia. Their clergy are also called priests and bishops. The leaders of the Church are called patriarchs.

An Orthodox Eucharist service is called the **Liturgy**. An important focus of the worship is the use of icons. Icons are religious paintings, usually of Jesus, the Virgin Mary, or one of the **saints**. The **iconostasis** ("place where icons are put") is the screen that divides all Orthodox churches in two. It has doors in the center. Only the priest goes through the doors, to the **altar** that is behind the screen. At certain times during an Orthodox service, the doors are opened, as a symbol that through Jesus it is possible to reach God.

Liberation theology

During the past 50 years or so, a new movement has become important in the Church, especially in Latin America. This is called Liberation **theology**. It is based on the idea that Christianity is about bringing good news to people who are poor and suffering. Liberation theologians believe that they should defend poor people against systems of government that keep a few people rich and powerful at the expense of most people. They remind people of Christian teachings, which some people living comfortable lives in rich countries have sometimes chosen to forget. Clergy in South America who have sided with poor people against corrupt governments have been killed. For example, Archbishop Oscar Romero was shot as he celebrated Mass in his cathedral in El Salvador.

Liberation theology has had an effect on the way that Church leaders in many countries view their responsibilities.

Protestant churches

Protestant churches include hundreds of Christian **denominations** (branches) all over the world. The largest are the Lutheran, Presbyterian, Episcopal, Methodist, and Baptist churches. All of these are Protestant, but each has its own way of worship. Generally, Protestant churches emphasize teaching from the Bible. They believe that individuals can make their own relationship with God through Jesus. Protestants believe that people are unable to save themselves because of their sins. Therefore, they are saved by the **grace** of God—not by the good things they do. Protestants also reject the idea that the pope should be the highest earthly authority. Most believe that the Bible should be the only authority for their religion.

A minister preaches at a Protestant church service.

About 380 million people belong to Protestant churches. The word "Protestant" comes from the Latin word "protestans," which means "one who protests." During the 1500s, many German leaders protested an attempt by Roman Catholics to limit the practice of Lutheranism. The leaders became known as Protestants (see page 11). The name soon came to include all Western Christians who had left the Roman Catholic Church. Most Protestants live in Europe and North America, but the number is increasing in areas such as Africa and Latin America.

The Bible

The Bible is the Christians' holy book. It is really a collection of 66 books put together and divided into two parts. The first part is the Old Testament, which includes most of the Jewish holy books. Jesus and all the first Christians were Jewish. Jewish teachings are included in the Bible because Christians consider them to be the word of God. The second part of the Bible is the New Testament. This is the story of Jesus and the early years of Christianity.

The Old Testament shows how the Jews gradually learned more about what God is like. Christians believe that it looks forward to the coming of Jesus as God's Messiah. Jews do not believe this, because they do not accept that Jesus was the Messiah.

The Old Testament

There are four groups of books in the Old Testament. The first group begins with the five books of teaching, which are about the beginning of the world and the early days of Judaism. Then, there are history books, which tell how the Jews developed as a nation. The third section consists of books of poetry, including the Book of Psalms, which is often used in Christian worship. The books that make up the largest group in the Old Testament are the books of the **prophets**. The prophets were messengers from God.

The New Testament

The New Testament is the story of the early years of Christianity. It begins with the four Gospels. "Gospel" comes from an old word that means "good news." The men who wrote the Gospels wanted to share what they believed was the good news about Jesus. They believed that he was the Son of God. Some stories appear in all four Gospels, but each writer chose to include the material that he thought was most important. The first three Gospels (Matthew, Mark, and Luke) are quite similar. John's Gospel is quite different, and most people agree that it was probably written later.

For many Christians, the family Bible is a treasured heirloom.

This illustration for the Book of Revelation is from a 16th-century Bible.

After the Gospels comes the Acts of the **Apostles**. This is the story of the first 50 or so years of Christianity. Much of Acts is about St. Paul and his preaching. Then, there are 21 letters, most of them written by St. Paul. He wrote to groups of Christian friends, teaching and advising them about how they should live. The letters are in the Bible because the advice they contain is important for every Christian, no matter when they live. The last book in the Bible is the book of Revelation, which is quite different from anything else in the New Testament. It was written to encourage Christians who were being persecuted by the Romans and tells of a series of visions that the author had. It is written in a sort of code, but contains some beautiful descriptions, especially about the end of the world and life after death.

Bible references

The Bible has been translated into over 2,000 different languages and into many different styles of English. There are enormous Bibles for reading in churches and tiny ones that can be worn as jewelry. Some are books that only contain part of the Bible. This could make it difficult to find a particular passage, because words that are on one page in one Bible may be on a totally different page in another Bible. To make it easier for readers to find their way around the Bible, every book has been divided into sections called chapters and smaller sections called verses. For example, one of the most famous verses in the Bible is, "God loved the world so much that he gave his only son, so that everyone who believes in him may not die, but have eternal life." This is in the Gospel of John, chapter 3, verse 16—usually written John 3:16. This is called the reference. Anyone looking for this verse, or any other, only needs to know the reference to be able to find it, no matter what the age, size, or language of the Bible.

Teachings of the Bible

Christians believe that the Bible is not just an ordinary book. They believe it is the word of God. Some Christians believe that the words it contains were literally given by God to the people who wrote them down. Most Christians today believe that it was inspired by God. In other words, the ideas that it contains came from God, but the words in which they were written down came from the people who wrote the books. These Christians obviously believe that the words themselves are less important than the ideas. In the same way, some Christians would argue that everything the Bible contains is fact. Others would argue that the Bible contains stories that teach important lessons about what God is like, but do not have to be something that really happened. An example of this is the story of the Creation. All Christians would agree that this story shows the power of God. Some Christians believe that it is a factual account, while others believe that it is a story that teaches important lessons.

The rest of the first chapter of Genesis continues the story of the first six days of the world, until the seventh day, when "God finished what he had been doing and stopped working."

The Creation

In the beginning, when God created the universe, the Earth was formless and desolate. The raging ocean that covered everything was engulfed in total darkness and the power of God was moving over the water. Then God commanded, "Let there be light" and light appeared. God was pleased with what he saw. Then he separated the light from the darkness and he named the light "Day" and the darkness "Night." Evening passed and morning came—that was the first day.
(Genesis 1:1–2)

The prophets

Christians believe that the books of the prophets teach important lessons about how God wants people to live. A famous passage is in the book of Micah, where the prophet says:

The Lord has told us what is good. What he requires of us is this: to do what is just, to show constant love, and to live in humble fellowship with our God. (Micah 7:8)

The New Testament

The four Gospels include different accounts of the things that Jesus did and what he taught. They were probably written about 40 years apart and by different people, so it would be very odd if they were all the same. The one miracle story that is in all four Gospels is the story of the Feeding of the Five Thousand. After explaining about the large crowd who had come to listen to Jesus teach, Luke's account goes on:

> They [the disciples] answered, "All we have are five loaves and two fish.
> Do you want us to go and buy food for this whole crowd?"
> [There were about 5,000 men there.]

> Jesus said to his disciples, "Make the people sit down in groups of about fifty each."
> After the disciples had done so, Jesus took the five loaves and two fish, looked up to
> heaven, thanked God for them, and gave them to the disciples to distribute to the people.
> They all ate and had enough, and the disciples took
> up twelve baskets of what was left over.
> (Luke 9:13–17)

Death and resurrection

By far the greatest part of all four Gospels is the story of the last week of Jesus' life. The writers obviously thought it was the most important part of their message.

In John's Gospel, the story of the resurrection is told like this:

> Early on Sunday morning, while it was still dark,
> Mary Magdalene went to the tomb and saw that the
> stone was taken away from the entrance. She went
> running to Simon Peter and the other disciple whom
> Jesus loved and told them, "They have taken away the
> Lord and we don't know where they have put him!"

> Then Peter and the other disciple went to the tomb.
> The two of them were running, but the other disciple
> ran faster than Peter and reached the tomb first. He
> bent over and saw the linen wrappings but he did
> not go in. Behind him came Simon Peter and he went
> straight into the tomb. He saw the linen wrappings
> lying there and the cloth that had been around Jesus'
> head. It was not lying with the linen wrappings but
> was rolled up by itself. Then the other disciple who
> had reached the tomb first also went in. He saw and
> believed. (John 20:1–8)

The resurrection is one of the most important parts of Christian teaching.

How Christians Worship

Christians often choose to worship in a church, which is a building set aside for the worship of God. However, they do not believe that this is the only place where they can worship. They believe that God is present everywhere, all the time, so everything they do can be part of their worship. This means that the way they live is very important.

Prayers

Worship at home takes many forms. Years ago, there were often formal family prayers every morning or evening, where everyone gathered in the same room and someone—usually the father—led everyone in prayer together. This may still happen in some families, but it is not very common today. Most Christians pray at home at a time and in a way that suits them. This may mean getting up early or setting aside a time before they go to bed. Sometimes Christians will use prayers that are written down in a book. Orthodox Christians have prayer books especially for use at home. At other times, Christians may make up a prayer of their own, telling God what they feel and asking for his help in their lives. Many Catholics pray using a Rosary. This is a string of beads, and a prayer is said for each bead. The prayers may be said aloud or silently.

The Lord's Prayer

One of the prayers that Christians use most often, at home and in church, is the prayer that Jesus taught his disciples. It is called the Lord's Prayer. It has been officially translated into 2,123 languages or dialects.

Our Father, who art in heaven,
hallowed be Thy name;
Thy kingdom come,
Thy will be done,
On Earth as it is in heaven.
Give us this day our daily bread;
And forgive us our trespasses,
As we forgive those who trespass
against us;
Lead us not into temptation,
but deliver us from evil,
For Thine is the kingdom,
the power, and the glory,
Forever. Amen.

Saying "grace," a prayer before meals, is part of worship at home for many Christians.

Bible study

Studying the Bible is something that all Christians feel is very important. Many Christians feel that in addition to reading the Bible in church, they want to get to know the Bible better by reading it at home. Several Christian organizations publish lists of Bible readings, often in a monthly cycle. The books also have notes attached to help people understand

A Bible-study group meets in the Philippines.

the passage they have read. Sometimes there are prayers, too, that are related to the reading. So, for example, if the Bible reading was about caring for others, the notes would explain details that a modern Christian might not understand. There may be a prayer asking God to bless people who are homeless or suffering from a natural disaster such as drought or flood.

Small groups

For some Christians, worshiping in a small group in which everyone knows each other is important. The people in a small group may worship together on a Sunday with a much larger congregation in a church. But at least once a week, they meet with their small group. Their group offers them a chance to develop their faith in a less formal way with their friends. They may sing modern religious songs, sometimes accompanied by a guitar. They may read the Bible and pray together. Meeting like this gives the group members a chance to discuss their attitudes, beliefs, and concerns with other people who have a similar religious outlook.

Our small group

Lizzie is 14 and lives with her family in Kent, England.

I belong to a young people's group, and we meet in somebody's house (we take turns being the host) every Thursday night. It's good because we all believe the same things. Some of my friends at school think I'm not normal when I say I'm a Christian, so it's easier to relax when I'm with the group. We pray together and talk about a Bible passage we've all read during the week. My favorite part is at the end when we all choose our favorite chorus to sing. Choruses are modern songs about Christianity. My favorite is "Open our eyes, Lord":

Open our eyes, Lord, for we would see Jesus,
To reach out and touch him and say that we love him,
Open our ears, Lord, and help us to listen,
Open our eyes, Lord, for we would see Jesus.

I like that because it's simple and it says what I want to say. Because some of the hymns we sing in church have such old words in them, I don't always understand them very well.

Worship in church

Christianity is made up of lots of different branches. Each one has particular beliefs or ways of worship that make it different from all the others. This means it is difficult to describe a "typical" Christian service. However, most Christians would recognize the descriptions here.

This priest is celebrating the Eucharist in a Roman Catholic church.

Christians may go to church at any time. They do not have to be with other people in order to worship. However, Christians have always believed that it is important to meet other Christians to worship together. Jesus once told his friends that "Where two or three come together in my name, I am there with them" (Matthew 18:20).

The most important day for group worship is Sunday. This is the first day of the week, and Christians worship then because they believe it is the day when Jesus rose from the dead. Saints' days and other festival days are often celebrated with special church services, too—especially in the Roman Catholic and Orthodox traditions.

Eucharist

In most churches (though not all), the Eucharist, or **Holy Communion**, is the most important celebration. Christians pray together, eat a small piece of bread or a special wafer (a thin disc of unleavened bread), and drink a little wine or grape juice. They do this to remember the Last Supper that Jesus ate with his disciples. At this meal, Jesus told them he was going to die. He gave the disciples bread and wine, saying that they were a symbol of his body and blood. He told the disciples that they should "Do this, to remember me." Ever since the earliest days of Christianity, Christians have celebrated this service to remember what Jesus said. They believe that because the bread and wine have been blessed, they have a special significance. Catholics and Orthodox believe that the body and blood of Christ are actually present in the Eucharist.

Singing hymns is an important part of many church services.

What happens in a church service?

In most churches, the general pattern of worship is the singing of religious songs called hymns or choruses, readings from the Bible, and prayers. During the service there is usually a talk by the priest, pastor, or other leader. This talk has different names in different churches. It may be called a sermon, a homily, or "the message." It is usually based on a reading from the Bible, often part of Jesus' teaching. The talk helps the people to understand more about the teaching and how it affects them in their lives.

Roman Catholic and Orthodox Christians use statues and candles as part of their worship. At some parts of the service, **incense** is used, too. At the heart of Catholic and Orthodox services are a prescribed set of prayers and chants and a systematic reading of the Bible, designed to praise God. Worship in **Pentecostal** or **charismatic** churches often includes bands, lively singing, dancing, and clapping. "Charisma" is a Greek word that means "gift," and the people in these churches believe that they can show God's gifts by doing the same amazing things that the first disciples did at Pentecost. During their services people may "speak in tongues" (sounds praising God that do not come from the person's normal language). People may be healed "in the name of Jesus." If someone needs particular help, there may be a laying on of hands, in which the leader or other person puts his or her hands on the person and prays for God to bless him or her. To show that they agree with what is being said or sung, the people often raise their hands above their heads and may shout, "Praise the Lord" or "Hallelujah."

Members of the Society of Friends, sometimes called Quakers, worship in a very different way. They do not have clergy. Their meetings—they do not call them services—take place in silence until one member of the group feels that God has given him or her something to say. They feel that this time of quiet and reflection gives them a breathing space and helps them to be Christians in a busy world.

Church Buildings

The word "church" is used in two ways. It can mean a group of Christian people—for example, the Methodist Church. It can also mean the building in which Christians worship. Like almost all other religions, from the earliest days, Christians have wanted special buildings in which to worship.

The earliest church of which anything remains is in Syria. It was built about 200 CE. Only the ruins are left, but these show that it was a normal house that was adapted so it could be used for worship. One room was used for worship and celebrating the Eucharist. Another was used for baptizing people. A third room may have been used as a classroom.

Cathedrals

The most important churches for Orthodox, Roman Catholic, and Protestant Christians are called cathedrals. A cathedral takes its name from the bishop's throne—the cathedra. Many cathedrals are very old and are beautifully decorated. Even today, many cathedrals are still the most impressive building in many cities. In the Middle Ages (c. 500 to 1500 CE), when most European cathedrals were built, ordinary people were very poor and lived in simple huts. The difference between these huts and the enormous, high, and beautifully decorated cathedrals must have been stunning. This helped to give ordinary people a sense of the importance of religion and worship.

Many elements in cathedral architecture, such as the high spires reaching toward the sky, are symbols of people's Christian faith.

Basilica-style churches

In the early days of Christianity, while Christians were being persecuted in the Roman Empire, special buildings were never used. Anyone going to one would have been assumed to be a Christian and arrested. It was only after Christianity became an accepted religion that churches began to be built. Christians copied the style of **basilicas**, the most important Roman buildings. They were rectangular and divided into three parts, with a higher central part. This is still the basic shape for many churches today, especially in Italy and southern Europe.

Cruciform churches

"Cruciform" means "cross-shaped." Traditionally, many churches were built in this shape as a reminder that Jesus was crucified. There are two main styles of cruciform churches. In Great Britain and northern Europe, it is common for churches to be cross-shaped (†). In eastern Europe, the "plus" shape (+) is more common. There is often a dome over the central part. This serves the same function as the tower, or spire, that is found in churches all over the world. It reminds the people that they should "look up" to God. Many churches have bells. This goes back to the days when most people did not have clocks, so the ringing bells reminded them that it was time for worship. Bells are also used for special occasions. A series of ringing bells celebrates a wedding, while a tolling bell (one bell rung slowly) is a sign of mourning at a funeral.

This Orthodox church is in Aegina, Greece.

Modern churches

In recent years, many different styles of church have been built. Some have been round or octagonal, so that everyone present can share in the worship and see easily. Some are built with removable seats so that the church rooms can be used for purposes other than worship. The church can be used for activities such as toddler groups and senior citizen lunches. In most churches where this is the case, the altar area, the holiest part of the church, can be screened off.

Saints

Many churches are dedicated to a saint or saints. The word "saint" can have different meanings among Christians. In some Protestant churches, any Christian can be a saint. Orthodox churches consider anyone who is in heaven to be a saint. Roman Catholics believe this, too, but also give special status (called canonization) to some people who were considered to be particularly close to God when they were alive. Many Christians believe that the saints help people to understand what God is like.

Inside church buildings

All churches are used for Christian worship, so they all contain some things that are the same. However, churches from different branches of Christianity can be quite different, since their members worship in different ways. For example, because there is a huge difference between worship in a large Orthodox church and worship in a small **Evangelical** church, the furnishings in each are different, too.

Altar

In most churches, the altar is the most important piece of furniture. It is the table used for the service of the Eucharist. In older churches, the altar is usually opposite the main entrance, in the area called the sanctuary. It may be separated from the rest of the church by a rail or stairs. This marks the difference between the sanctuary, the holiest part of the church, and the nave, where the people sit. In Orthodox churches, the altar is separated from the main body of the church by the main screen—the iconostasis. An altar may be made of wood or stone and is sometimes beautifully carved. In some churches the altar is called the Communion Table. It is generally more plain and simple and has a raised area in front of it where people may kneel to receive the bread and wine at the Eucharist.

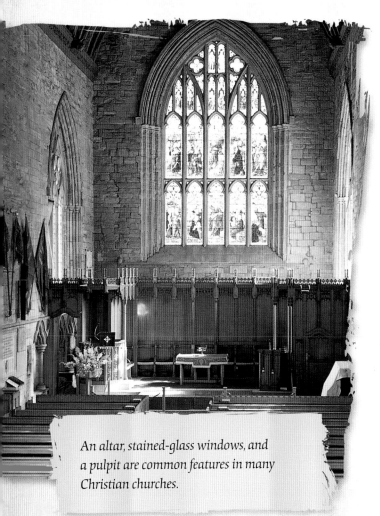

An altar, stained-glass windows, and a pulpit are common features in many Christian churches.

Pulpit

In some churches, the **pulpit** is an enclosed, raised area, usually near the front or at the side of a church. In older churches, it may be reached by climbing a short flight of steps. In some Protestant denominations, the pulpit is the most noticeable part of the church and is used by the person leading the worship for the whole service. In other churches, the pulpit is only used by the person who is giving the sermon, the special talk that is an important part of most services.

Font

The **font** is a special bowl that holds the water used in the service of baptism. The bowl is placed in a carved stand, usually made of wood or stone. In some churches it is near the door, a symbol that baptism is the entry to the Church. Some churches baptize by **total immersion**, when the person's whole

Christian symbols

The most common symbol in Christianity is a cross. This is a reminder that Jesus was killed by being crucified. A cross with a figure of Jesus on it is called a crucifix. The fish symbol is also used. Many of the earliest Christians were fishermen, and Jesus once said, "I will make you fishers of men." Also, in Greek, the word for fish is "ICHTHUS (ΙΧΘΥΣ)." The letters of this word match the first letters of the Greek words "Iesous Christos Theou Uios Soter" ("Jesus Christ, God's son, Savior"). This sums up the most important things that Christians believe. Other Greek letters are sometimes used. Jesus is sometimes represented by Alpha and Omega (ΑΩ), the first and last letters of the Greek alphabet, to show that he was there at the beginning and will be there at the end of time.

body is immersed under the water. A font would not be large enough for this type of baptism, so in Orthodox and Baptist churches there is usually a part of the floor that can be used as a pool. This is called a **baptistry**.

Decorations

Churches have many different sorts of decoration. In Orthodox churches, the pictures of the saints—icons— are very important. In Roman Catholic churches, there are usually statues of Jesus, Mary, and the saints. There are often paintings on the walls that tell the story of the crucifixion. These are called the Stations of the Cross and are used especially during the weeks before Easter services, called **Lent**. Many churches use candles and lamps for decoration. This may be a symbol of Jesus as "the Light of the World," one of the titles that Christians give him. Stained glass in the windows helps to make the church beautiful and can also be used to tell stories from the Bible.

Candles, the cross, and fish are all Christian symbols.

St. Peter's, Rome

Christianity is the largest religion in the world. It has followers in almost every country, all with different styles of churches. Rome has been a center of Christianity from a very early stage in the religion's history. St. Peter may well have lived and died there, and many people believe that St. Paul was killed in Rome during the persecution under the Emperor Nero, around 62 CE. Today, the Vatican in Rome is the headquarters of the Roman Catholic Church. The Vatican Palace, where the pope lives, contains over 1,000 rooms. One of the most famous is the Sistine Chapel. The ceiling in this room was painted by Michelangelo between 1508 and 1512. His paintings are said to be among the finest works of art that have ever been produced. The main church in the Vatican is the Basilica of St. Peter. The first church on this site almost certainly dated from the 3rd century CE. The present building was completed between the 15th and 17th centuries. It is one of the largest churches in the world and is full of paintings and other treasures.

St. Peter's Basilica in Rome is one of the most impressive churches in the world.

The Patriarchal Cathedral of the Epiphany, Moscow

This cathedral is one of the most important and most beautiful Orthodox churches in Russia. The iconostasis is covered in gold and is very richly decorated. The walls are decorated with paintings and icons, and there is a splendid chandelier. Like all Orthodox churches, there are no seats—people stand to worship. The richness of the decorations is a

Creeds

Whichever branch they belong to and wherever they worship, Christians use creeds—statements that sum up their beliefs. The simplest and oldest Christian creed is "Jesus is Lord," which was used in the earliest days of the Church. As time went on, creeds included more beliefs, and so they became more complex. The Apostles' Creed, named after the early Christian preachers, has been used for hundreds of years. It is still used in many services today. It begins, "I believe in God, the Father Almighty, maker of heaven and earth, and in Jesus Christ, his only Son, our Lord . . ."

symbol of the majesty of God. It also contrasts with the simplicity of the outside of the building. Orthodox Christians say that this difference between the inside and outside of their churches is a symbol of the difference between this life and the new world to come.

The Crystal Cathedral, California

One of the most unusual churches in the world is the Crystal Cathedral in Garden Grove, California. This modern building is made almost entirely of glass. There are 10,000 panes of glass in the walls and the ceiling! They cover a weblike steel frame. This allows worshipers to see the beauty of the world outside. There are also two doors almost 100 feet (30 meters) high, which can be opened to allow an even better view. Many Christians believe that they can worship God through the beauty of what he has created. Every year in this church, there are two special celebrations. At the Glory of Christmas and the Glory of Easter, people, animals, and amazing special effects bring the Gospel to life. The Crystal Cathedral is also famous for its music—especially the organ it is played upon. This is the largest one of its type ever built and has 17,000 pipes!

The Crystal Cathedral in California is built almost entirely of glass.

The Yoido Full Gospel Church, Korea

The Yoido Full Gospel Church in Korea belongs to the Pentecostal group of churches. It is a modern building that is not particularly beautiful or richly decorated. It is famous because it has the largest worshiping congregation of any church in the world. Over 750,000 people are members of this one church. This is one example that shows how the Pentecostal movement has grown to become a very important part of Christianity in the 21st century.

Pilgrimage

A **pilgrim** is someone who makes a journey because of his or her religion. Pilgrims believe that by going on a **pilgrimage**, they will in some way become closer to God. Some Christians believe that going on a pilgrimage and asking for forgiveness means that God is more likely to forgive their sins. Sometimes pilgrims want to make a special prayer, and hope that it will be more powerful if it is made at the **shrine** of a particular saint. Other pilgrims may want to offer thanks to a saint because a prayer has been answered. All pilgrims share the belief that the pilgrimage is an important part of their worship.

Places of Christian pilgrimage

There are thousands of places all over the world that are important for Christians. Hundreds of thousands of Christians visit Israel every year. They go to Jerusalem, Bethlehem, and Galilee and can feel that they are in the places that Jesus knew when he was alive on Earth. Many pilgrims visit churches like the Church of the **Nativity** in Bethlehem, which is said to be built on the site of the stable where Jesus was born. Similarly, the Church of the Holy Sepulcher is said to be built at the site of the cave-tomb where Jesus' body was buried.

This simple stone altar is in the Church of the Holy Sepulcher, Jerusalem. The church is said to be on the site where Jesus' body was buried after the crucifixion.

Our Lady of Guadalupe

In 1531 Juan Diego, a peasant farmer in what is now Mexico, saw a vision of the Virgin Mary. She told him to build a church where she was standing. No one believed the farmer, but the figure appeared again and offered proof. Roses bloomed on the hillside, even though it was December. A picture of the Virgin's face also appeared on Juan Diego's cloak. This picture still exists today, and scientists have not been able to discover how it got onto the material. Juan Diego took the roses and his cloak to the local bishop to prove what he had seen. The bishop was convinced, and a church was built. It has been a center of pilgrimage ever since. Today, 10 million people visit the shrine in Mexico City every year. It is second only to the Vatican in popularity.

Lourdes

Lourdes is in southwestern France. It is a particular center of pilgrimage for people who are sick or disabled. Its importance comes from the visions of a young girl named Bernadette Soubirous. She said that between February 11 and July 16, 1858, she saw and talked with the Virgin Mary 18 times. On February 25, 1859, a spring was discovered at the spot where Bernadette said the Virgin had stood. Scientists cannot detect special properties in the water, but many people claim that drinking it has benefited them. Every year, some of the 70,000 people who go to Lourdes claim that they have been healed in some way. Some people claim they have been cured of their cancer or that they no longer need a wheelchair. The Roman Catholic Church investigates all these claims carefully. For other people, the benefit is more to do with spiritual healing. Almost everyone who goes to Lourdes says that they have been moved in some way by their visit.

The statue of Christ the Redeemer overlooks Rio de Janeiro, in Brazil.

José's view

José is 14 and lives in Rio de Janeiro, Brazil.

I can see the statue from the windows at the front of my house. Every time I look at it, I know that I'm looking at one of the most famous views in our city, and probably in the world. The statue shows Jesus with his hands raised, blessing the city. We often think that our city needs looking after and helping! People come from all over the world to visit Rio, and some of them are pilgrims who go up the mountain to get a closer look at the statue. But I'm lucky—I can see it all the time. It makes me feel good when I look at it, because it reminds me that Jesus is always with me.

Celebrations

Children often take part in Nativity plays at Christmas.

Christmas has become a national holiday in many parts of the world and is a special time for many people who are not Christians. It is important to remember that many "Christmas customs" have little to do with Christianity. Many customs started with a religious meaning, but now they have more to do with tradition than religion.

Advent

Advent is the season that begins the Christian year. The word "Advent" comes from a Latin word that means "coming." Christians look forward to the coming of Jesus, celebrated at Christmas, and they remember the belief that Jesus will come again to begin a new kingdom on Earth. Many Christians use Advent calendars and candles as ways of showing that Christmas is getting closer. Advent calendars have small windows to open each day, revealing a tiny picture beneath. Advent candles have sections that can be burned each day.

Cathy's view

Cathy is 12 and lives in Western Australia.

Christmas is a mixture of old and new in our house. We still get a lot of the traditional stuff like snow scenes on Christmas cards, but for us Christmas is in the middle of summer. We usually have a really lazy day. It starts on Christmas Eve when we go to church for Midnight Mass. This is always a special service, but I must admit I'm sometimes nearly asleep by the time it finishes! On Christmas Day us kids usually wake up early and we always find our presents under the tree. Sometimes we go to church again on Christmas morning. We have our main meal at lunchtime, and Mom usually cooks some seafood on the barbecue. We have cold meats and salad and things like that. Everybody eats too much! In our town, Father Christmas [Santa Claus] comes around on a pickup truck on Christmas afternoon. He usually wears shorts because it's so hot. He gives out candies to the kids. We usually have visitors in the evening. If my cousins come, we show off our presents to each other. It all makes a special day, but in our family we think it's most special because we've been to church and remembered what Christmas is really all about.

Christmas

The word "Christmas" comes from "Christ's mass," the church service held to celebrate Jesus' birth. Christmas has been celebrated on December 25 since about 300 CE. This is not the actual date on which Jesus born—no one knows when that was. The early Christians adopted December 25 because it was already a festival. The difference in calendars between the Western and Orthodox churches means that most Orthodox Christians celebrate Christmas on January 6.

Many Christians go to Midnight Mass on Christmas Eve. It is held around midnight because Christians believe that Jesus was born during the night. Services are also held on Christmas morning. The services thank God for the gift of his son, Jesus. There are readings from the Bible about the birth of Jesus, and people sing special hymns, often traditional songs called carols. The word "carol" comes from an old French word that means "dance." Hundreds of years ago, people used to dance around the church as they were singing.

Nativity scenes

Nativity scenes are an important part of the Christmas decorations in many countries in the world. They show the traditional idea of the Nativity, the scene in the stable when Jesus was born. They include Mary, Joseph, shepherds, wise men, an angel, and the animals in the stable. The most important figure, baby Jesus, is always shown lying in a manger. Nativity scenes range from tiny ones, which can be put on a mantelpiece, to almost life-size figures in churches or shopping centers.

A traditional Nativity scene shows Jesus shortly after his birth in a stable.

Epiphany

"**Epiphany**" means "showing." In Western Christianity, it is on January 6. It reminds Christians of the story in Matthew's Gospel about how Jesus was shown to the wise men who had traveled to see him. In Orthodox churches that celebrate Christmas Day on January 6, Epiphany is on January 19. Orthodox Christians celebrate Epiphany as a time to remember when Jesus was baptized and was shown to be the Son of God.

Lent

Lent, the church season before Easter, is the most solemn time of the Christian year. It reminds Christians of the time when, according to the Bible, Jesus spent 40 days in the desert after his baptism, thinking and praying about the work he believed God wanted him to do. The day before Lent begins is called Shrove Tuesday in some cultures. "Shrove" is an old English word that means "being forgiven for things you have done wrong." Catholics go to confession as part of Lent. They tell the priest the things that they had done wrong, so that he can give them absolution (forgiveness) and tell them what to do to show they are truly sorry. They can then begin Lent with a clear conscience. In some places, the day before Lent is called Mardi Gras, or "Fat Tuesday." In many cultures, people will give up sweets or fatty things for Lent. They use up all those foods on the Tuesday before Lent begins. In the Orthodox Church, Lent is a time of strict **fasting**.

Decorated eggs are an Easter custom.

The first day of Lent is called Ash Wednesday. Its name comes from the special service that some branches of Christianity hold on this day. The priest or pastor uses ashes left from burning palm leaves to make the sign of the cross on a person's forehead. This reminds Christians that they will all die someday.

Easter

Easter is the most important and the most joyful Christian festival. Christians remember Jesus' death and celebrate his resurrection. The week before Easter is called Holy Week. It begins on Palm

Easter eggs

Celebrating Easter with eggs is a very old custom. Eggs have been thought to be special since long before the time of Jesus. Outside, they are hard, dry, and apparently dead. But they contain life inside them. After the first Easter, Christians began to think of them as a symbol of the tomb from which the resurrected Jesus had broken out, in the same way that a chick bursts out of the shell. So, eggs have always been part of Easter celebrations. In some places, eggs are dyed with different colors or decorated in some other way. Years ago, it was the custom to give carved eggs made of wood or even precious stones as presents. Then came the idea of making imitation eggs to eat. At first, they were made of marzipan or sugar. In the last 200 years, chocolate eggs have become popular.

Sunday, when Christians remember Jesus riding into Jerusalem, where crowds of people celebrated his coming as they waved palm leaves. Maundy Thursday was the day on which Jesus ate the Last Supper with his disciples. Its name comes from the Latin word "mandatum," meaning "command." At the meal, Jesus told his friends he was giving them a new commandment—to love one another. In many churches, all of the candles, linens, and other objects around the altar are removed or covered with a cloth at the end of Maundy Thursday through Good Friday.

Good Friday is the most solemn day of the year. Christians remember that Jesus was crucified. They believe that because Jesus died, the barriers between people and God were removed and their sins can be forgiven. This is why it is called "Good" Friday, even though it was the day Jesus died. Solemn church services are held, especially around three o' clock in the afternoon, which the Gospels say is the time Jesus died.

Easter Sunday services celebrate the belief that Jesus rose out of the tomb and was seen alive by his friends. Christians believe that he is still alive today, although not on Earth and not in a human body. They believe that the resurrection shows that death is not the end, but rather a new beginning of life with God. In some churches, services are held around midnight, because Christians believe that the resurrection happened during the night. This service is called the Easter vigil. Elaborate services are held during the day on Easter Sunday.

In the Orthodox Church, the Easter services are especially important. They are centered on the belief in Jesus as "the Light of the World." A special service is held at midnight as Easter Day begins. The church is in darkness, to show that Jesus is in the tomb. The priest comes out from behind the iconostasis with a lighted candle, and all the people light their candles from his. The church gradually fills with light. This is a symbol that the Light of the World has returned.

At Orthodox services on Easter eve, the priest comes out from behind the iconostasis with a lighted candle.

Pentecost

Christians celebrate Pentecost 50 days after Easter with special services. In some churches, it is a special day to have baptisms or **confirmations**, which are ceremonies when people join the Church. This is perhaps where Pentecost's other name, "Whit Sunday," came from. The name was probably once White Sunday because, years ago, many people were baptized on this day and wore white clothes for the ceremony.

What the Bible says about Pentecost

In the Bible, Luke talks of the day of the Jewish festival of Pentecost, seven weeks after the festival of Passover, which was when Jesus had been crucified. According to Luke, on this day, the followers of Jesus heard a noise like a rushing wind filling the house. They saw what looked like tongues of flame resting on the head of each person there. They were totally changed from the people who had been terrified and in hiding. They rushed outside and soon attracted the attention of a large crowd. They were speaking in different languages, which Luke says the foreign Jews in the crowd understood. Many of the crowd thought that Jesus' followers were drunk, but Peter, their spokesman, said that this was not true. He began telling the crowd what the followers believed about Jesus and the work he had done. The Bible says that on that day, 3,000 people became followers of Jesus.

Red and white are the colors of Pentecost.

What do Christians believe happened at Pentecost?

Many Christians believe that the story of Pentecost in the Acts of the Apostles is a straightforward account of the events that happened. Other Christians believe that the account does not describe a real wind or real fire. They point out that the power of God is often described as fire or wind in the Jewish Scriptures, or holy books, and this may be why Luke used that description. Many Christians believe that the disciples talked in foreign languages that the people listening could understand. Other Christians prefer to think that the disciples were tremendously excited, and it was their excitement that the crowd understood, rather than the exact words.

Whatever they believe about what happened, all Christians would agree that the important thing about Pentecost was the effect that it had on the followers. They had been men and women who were hiding, afraid that they were going to be killed. They were changed into people who were prepared to go out and tell anyone who wanted to listen about what they believed.

How Christians celebrate Pentecost

Christians believe that the events of Pentecost were so important because it was the real beginning of the Christian Church. Every year at Pentecost there are special church services. In many places Christians go on processions through the local area as a way of showing what they believe. This reminds everyone that Christians believe that the same Holy Spirit that was given to the first disciples at Pentecost is still working in the world today.

A Pentecost procession takes place in Seville, Spain.

The World Council of Churches

Pentecost is often an occasion when different churches work together—for example, by joining together in processions. In the last 50 years, events like joint church services between different branches of Christianity have become much more common. A formal way for Christians to work together is the World Council of Churches (WCC). This was formed in 1948. The idea of greater cooperation among churches first came from Christian missionaries. They found that the people they were preaching to were confused by the differences between the churches. Today, the WCC claims to represent 400 million Christians all over the world, including members of 300 different branches. The idea is not to make all Christians belong to one huge church. Each branch has its own way of doing things and is special to its members. However, increasing the amount of contact between the churches means that everyone benefits. They can appreciate the different traditions and different ways of looking at the religion without losing their own uniqueness.

Family Occasions

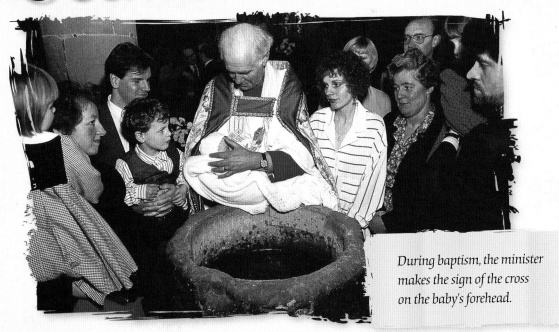

During baptism, the minister makes the sign of the cross on the baby's forehead.

Baptism—sometimes called Christening—is the special service held when someone joins the Church. In many branches of Christianity, the person being baptized is a baby. Sometimes it is the service at which a baby is officially given his or her name. The baby's parents bring the baby to church along with two or three other relatives or friends who are called godparents or sponsors. The adults promise to bring the child up to follow Jesus.

Baptism usually takes place as part of a normal church service. At the beginning of the ceremony, the baby, parents, and godparents gather around the font. This contains water that has been specially blessed. The minister holds the baby. He or she uses water from the font to make the sign of the cross on the baby's forehead, saying, "I baptize you in the name of the Father, and of the Son, and of the Holy Spirit."

Believers' baptism

Several branches of Christianity do not baptize babies. The largest is the Baptist Church. They have a service of blessing for babies, but feel that baptism should wait until people can make the promises for themselves. In these churches, baptism usually takes place by total immersion, when the person's whole body is placed under the water. The minister asks questions about the person's beliefs, and he or she declares a belief in Jesus and apologizes for any sins. The minister then lowers the person gently backward, so that he or she is under the water for a few seconds. This is a symbol that all sins are being washed away.

Orthodox churches

Orthodox churches always baptize by total immersion. The priest holds the baby and says, "The servant of God [baby's name] is baptized in the name of the Father. Amen. And of the Son. Amen. And of the Holy Spirit. Amen." As each person of the Trinity is mentioned, the baby is immersed under the water. For adult baptism, the baptistry is used, if the church has one, or a container that is large enough to immerse the person in is brought into the church. Immediately after the baptism, the person is Chrismated. This means that the priest uses a special oil to make the sign of the cross on the person's forehead, eyes, nostrils, mouth, ears, chest, hands, and feet. Each time, the priest says, "The seal of the gift of the Holy Spirit." After this ceremony, the person—baby or adult— is counted as being a full member of the Church and can receive Holy Communion.

Confirmation

Confirmation is the service held for people to "confirm" (make stronger) the promises that were made on their behalf when they were baptized. In most churches, it is held when someone is a teenager, but there is no age limit. In Orthodox churches, it is part of baptism. Christians believe that at the confirmation service, the person receives the gifts of the Holy Spirit. The bishop, priest, or pastor lays hands on the person's head and asks God to bless him or her. The person answers questions about his or her faith and is usually given a Bible or prayer book.

The sacraments

For most Christians, the sacraments are the most important services in which they receive blessings from God. However, different branches have different ideas. Catholics and Orthodox Christians believe there are seven sacraments and that the sacraments are powerful, visible signs of Christ that will transform the recipient. In contrast, Protestants accept only two (baptism and Holy Communion). They believe the sacraments are external signs only. They believe that the real powerful change takes place inside the person's heart and mind by belief alone, not by means of a visible, physical action.

People being confirmed have sponsors who help them prepare.

Marriage

Marriage is a sacrament, or solemn observance. It is also a legal ceremony. In all marriage services, certain sentences have to be said by law, and the ceremony must be made in front of at least two witnesses. While it is not required, most Christians choose to marry in a church, because they want a religious dimension to the service.
For Christians, making their **vows** in "God's house" is important. The Bible says that marriage was given by God so that men and women could be joined together for life and help each other.

A couple celebrate a traditional church wedding.

In a Western church wedding, the marriage begins with the priest, pastor, or other leader saying that everyone is gathered there in God's presence to witness the couple's marriage. The couple declare that they do not know any reason why they should not marry each other. They promise to live together and love each other and no one else. As a sign of the promises, the bridegroom gives the bride a ring that she wears on the fourth finger of her left hand. The bride may give the bridegroom a ring, too, that he wears on the same finger. There are prayers asking God to bless the couple. At the end of the service, the bride and groom and at least two witnesses sign the marriage certificate. In many branches of Christianity, the marriage may include a service of the Eucharist.

Orthodox weddings

The service in Orthodox churches is similar and must include the words that are required by law. But in the second part of the service, after they have exchanged rings, the couple receive crowns to wear. In the Russian Orthodox Church, these are made of silver or gold.

Rose's view

Rose is 14 and lives in New Jersey.

I went to my cousin Mary's wedding last year. The wedding was in the church her family goes to, and there were lots of flowers. It looked beautiful. As the guests came in, all of them were given a special candleholder and a candle to put in it. They all lit the candles and put them on the table at the front. Then, when Mary and Zak lit the Unity Candle to show they were becoming one, all the candles burned together. It looked very pretty. Afterward, the guests all got to take their candleholders away with them. It was like a memento of the day. Mary and Zak had written their own vows for part of the service, and everyone said it was good that it made what they said special for them. Lots of people cried, but I didn't!

In the Greek Orthodox Church, they are made of leaves and flowers. They are a symbol of God's blessing on the couple. At the end of the service, the couple drink wine from the same cup. This is a symbol of the life they will share together.

Divorce

Christianity teaches that a marriage should last until death. However, some churches accept that sometimes this does not happen and that there are circumstances in which prolonging a marriage may be more damaging than ending it. All churches teach that every effort should be made to rebuild a marriage that has broken down. This is particularly important if there are children involved.

This priest is conducting a Greek Orthodox wedding ceremony.

Death and beyond

Death has become a subject that many people prefer not to think about, especially in Western countries. Even though it happens to everyone, it has become "unmentionable," and most people choose to live pretending that it will never happen to them. This attitude affects Christians, too, but Christianity teaches that death is not the end, but rather the beginning of a new life with God.

Christian funerals

The service held when someone dies is a funeral. A Christian funeral is a time of hope as well as sadness. People are sad because the person they loved is no longer with them. They usually wear black or dark clothes as a sign of this. There are prayers that entrust the soul of the person who has died to God and that ask God to look after the people who are left behind. The hymns and Bible readings at the funeral, however, emphasize the hope that Christians have. They speak of Jesus as the Resurrection and the Life, and look forward to a time when all Christians will be reunited with people they have loved who have "gone before."

After the service, the body is either buried or **cremated**. A burial includes a short service by the grave, and the coffin is lowered into the ground using ropes. The earth is replaced into the grave after the people have left. In Western countries, cremation is becoming more common. A body is burned at a very high temperature in a special oven. The ashes left from cremation may be scattered or buried. The place where a body or ashes are buried is usually marked with a gravestone or a plaque. This may have the name of the person carved on it, with the dates that he or she lived and details of relatives or other important aspects of the person's life.

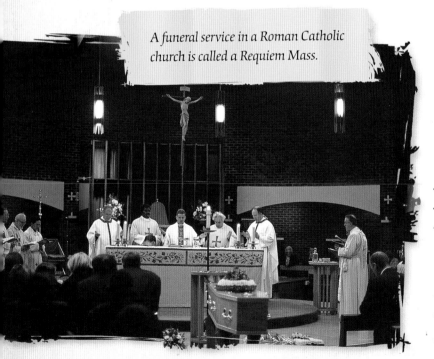

A funeral service in a Roman Catholic church is called a Requiem Mass.

After death

Christianity teaches that after death, the soul lives on. At some stage in the future (different branches of Christianity do not agree about when this will be), there will be a Day of Judgment. On that day, Christians believe Jesus will return as King and Judge, and everyone will be judged as to how they lived on Earth. At this time, in some miraculous way, they will be reunited with their bodies. In the past, the teaching about what happened next was simple and straightforward. People who had lived a good life would go to heaven—a place of light and peace usually pictured as being above the clouds. People who had been bad would go to hell. This was a place of burning fire and torment, with devils and everlasting torture.

This is the traditional teaching, which is found in the Bible. Most Christians today believe that this is what will happen at the Day of Judgment. They justify it because, through the teachings of Jesus, God has warned people what will happen. They say that if people refuse to believe in the teachings while they have the opportunity, they will have no one to blame but themselves. However, there are also Christians today who find it difficult to think of a loving God condemning people to burn in hell forever. Their beliefs suggest more vaguely that heaven is a state of being with God, and hell is the state of being away from God.

This 15th-century painting shows the Day of Judgment.

𝔄 Christian view of death

This extract is sometimes read at Christian funerals. It was written about 100 years ago by Henry Scott Holland, who was a clergyman:

Death is nothing at all. I have only slipped away into the next room. I am I, and you are you. Whatever we were to each other, that we still are. Call me by my old familiar name, speak to me in the easy way which you always used. Put no difference in your tone, wear no forced air of solemnity or sorrow. Laugh as we always laughed at the little jokes we enjoyed together. Play, smile, think of me, pray for me. Let my name be ever the household word that it always was, let it be spoken without effort, without the trace of shadow on it. Life means all that it ever meant. It is the same as it ever was; there is unbroken continuity. Why should I be out of mind because I am out of sight? I am waiting for you, for an interval, somewhere very near, just around the corner. All is well.

What It Means to Be a Christian

Respecting and helping other people is an important part of Christian teaching.

As individuals

Christianity teaches that Jesus' death was for all people, but that every individual needs to make a personal commitment to follow Jesus. Like the followers of every religion, Christians are individuals, and they do not all see their religion in the same way. Being a Christian may mean being a monk or a **nun** whose whole life is dedicated to worship, or being someone who only attends church occasionally but tries to follow Jesus' teachings in his or her life.

Most Christians believe that it is important to know the Bible and to follow its teachings. Since they try to follow the example of Jesus in their lives, it is important to get to know the things that he said and did. Many Christians study the Bible regularly. Most feel that it is important to meet and share their beliefs with other Christians in order to learn more about their faith and understand it better.

Nuns and monks

Some Christians feel that God wants them to live in a special way. In some churches—particularly the Orthodox and Roman Catholic churches—Christians can dedicate their whole lives to God. They are called nuns and monks. Most nuns and monks live in communities where everyone follows the same way of living. These communities are called Orders. When they join the Order, monks and nuns take vows about how they will live. The three most common vows are poverty (they have no possessions of their own), celibacy (they will not marry), and obedience (they will obey the head of their Order). Some Orders are cloistered (enclosed), so their members spend all their time away from "the world," concentrating on prayer and worship. Other Orders work with other people, usually in jobs like teaching and nursing.

In the community

One of the teachings of Jesus on which Christians base their attitude toward other people is the Parable of the Sheep and the Goats (Matthew 25:31–36). In this story, Jesus taught that at the Day of Judgment, the Son of Man will send to eternal punishment the "goats" who have not cared for other people: "Whenever you refused to help one of these least important ones, you refused to help me."

Many Christians care for other people. It may be just helping someone they know, or it may be more formal. Christian charities like Christian Aid and the Church World Service work in many countries with people of all faiths and none. They try to improve the conditions in which people have to live and work. Other organizations like the Salvation Army and Teen Challenge work in countries all over the world to help people with drug addiction problems.

In the world

In recent years, many Christians have become increasingly concerned about environmental matters and the damage human beings are doing to the planet. This is connected to the Christian idea of stewardship. A steward is someone who looks after something that will eventually be returned to its owner. It is becoming increasingly clear to people of all religions that the world cannot go on as it is, and many Christians today are becoming concerned about their effect on the world. This is particularly true of people who live in rich Western countries, who consume far more than their share of the world's resources, leaving people in poorer countries to suffer. This goes against Christian teaching about caring for others.

For similar reasons, Christians all over the world are concerned about the effects of war and violence. Many Christians see it as part of their Christian duty to work for peace, although some believe that war may be necessary in some circumstances.

Nuns and monks often work in the community in ways that help other people.

Map

The globe on the right shows the location of the map below.

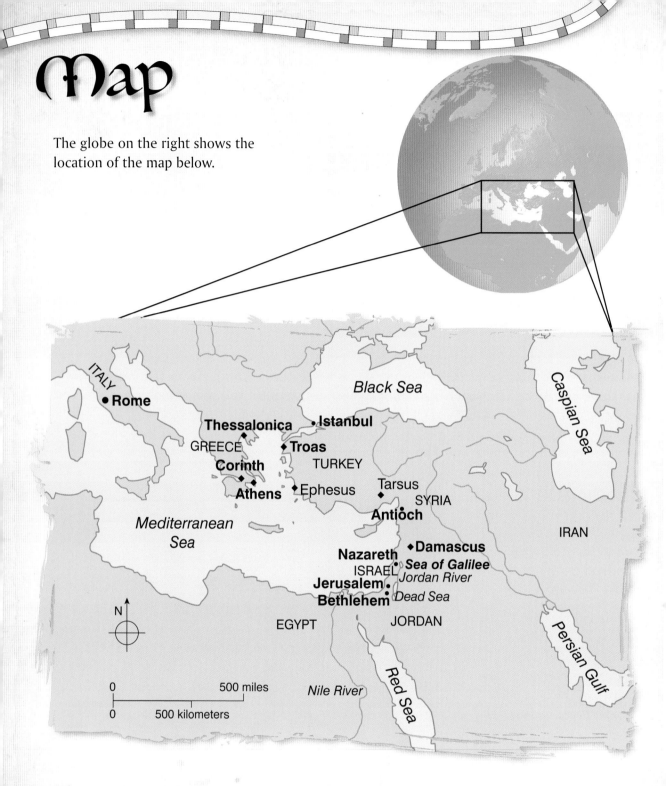

Place names

Some places on this map, or mentioned in the book, are called by different names today:

Constantinople—Istanbul

Palestine—Israel

◆ These are some of the places mentioned in the stories about St. Paul's missionary journeys.

Timeline

Major events in world history

BCE	3000–1700	Indus valley civilization flourishes
	2500	Pyramids in Egypt built
	1800	Stonehenge completed
	1220	Rameses II builds the Temple of Amon (Egypt)
	1000	Nubian Empire (countries around the Nile) begins and lasts until c. 350 CE
	776	First Olympic Games
	450s	Greece is a center of art and literature under Pericles
	336–323	Conquests of Alexander the Great
	300	Mayan civilization begins
	200	Great Wall of China begun
	48	Julius Caesar becomes Roman emperor
CE	79	Eruption of Vesuvius destroys Pompeii
	161–80	Golden Age of the Roman Empire under Marcus Aurelius
	330	Byzantine Empire begins
	868	First printed book (China)
	c. 1000	Leif Ericson may have discovered America
	1066	Battle of Hastings; Norman Conquest of Britain
	1300	Ottoman Empire begins (lasts until 1922)
	1325	Aztec Empire begins (lasts until 1521)
	1400	Black Death kills one person in three throughout China, North Africa, and Europe
	1452	Leonardo da Vinci born
	1492	Christopher Columbus sails to America
	1564	William Shakespeare born
	1620	Pilgrims arrive in what is now Massachusetts
	1648	Taj Mahal built
	1768–71	Captain Cook sails to Australia
	1776	Declaration of Independence
	1859	Charles Darwin publishes *Origin of Species*
	1908	Henry Ford produces the first Model T Ford car
	1914–18	World War I
	1929	Wall Street Crash and the Great Depression
	1939–45	World War II
	1946	First computer invented
	1953	Chemical structure of DNA discovered
	1969	First moon landings
	1981	AIDS virus diagnosed
	1984	Scientists discover a hole in the ozone layer
	1989	Berlin Wall is torn down
	1991	Breakup of the former Soviet Union
	1994	Nelson Mandela becomes president of South Africa
	1997	An adult mammal, Dolly the sheep, is cloned for the first time
	2000	Millennium celebrations take place all over the world

Major events in Christian history

BCE	c. 4	Jesus of Nazareth born
CE	c. 30	Jesus of Nazareth crucified
	40	One of the earliest Christian churches is founded at Corinth
	45	St. Paul begins his missionary journeys
	58	St. Paul's letters to the Corinthians
	64	Christians are persecuted under Roman Emperor Nero
	c. 65–110	Gospels written
	c. 251–350	Life of St. Anthony, the first Christian monk
	302	Massive persecution of Christians under Roman Emperor Diocletian
	313	Roman Emperor Constantine the Great becomes a Christian
	325	First formal creed established
	347–419	St. Jerome first translates Bible into Latin
	529	St. Benedict of Nursia founds the first monastery
	596	Augustine becomes first archbishop of Canterbury
	c. 700	*Lindisfarne Gospels* written
	1054	The Great Schism—split between Eastern and Western churches
	1095–1204	The Crusades—European Christians battle with Muslim soldiers in the eastern Mediterranean to conquer the Holy Land
	1182–1226	St. Francis of Assisi
	1382	Followers of John Wycliffe first translate the Bible into English
	1390–1440	*Imitation of Christ*, an influential devotional book, is written, perhaps by Thomas à Kempis
	1517	Martin Luther pins his protest to church door at Wittenberg
	1525	First English Bible printed by William Tyndale
	1531	Juan Diego has vision of the Virgin Mary in Mexico
	1545–63	Council of Trent, a meeting of high-level members of the Roman Catholic Church, reforms and clarifies Church teachings. As a result, Roman Catholicism is revitalized.
	1611	*King James* version of the Bible printed
	1620	Puritan colony established in America
	1624–91	George Fox (founder of the Society of Friends, also known as Quakers)
	1639	First U.S. Baptist church
	1703–91	John Wesley (Christian preacher and founder of Methodism)
	1784	First U.S. Methodist church
	1787	African Methodist Episcopal Church founded in New York
	1858	Bernadette Soubirous has visions of Virgin Mary at Lourdes, France
	1899	Gideon's International begins to distribute Bibles to hotels all over the world
	1948	Founding of the World Council of Churches
	1976	*Good News Bible* published

Glossary

Advent	weeks before Christmas; first season of the Christian year
altar	table used for the service of Holy Communion
angel	messenger from God
Apostles	one of Christ's 12 original followers
ascension	term used by Christians to describe Jesus going up into heaven
baptism	sacrament in which someone becomes a child of God and a member of the Church
baptistry	small pool in a church floor used for baptism; also the area in a church where baptisms take place
basilica	important Roman building, now used as a name for a type of church built in the same style
Bible	Christians' holy book; the word of God
bishop	senior priest
blasphemy	saying insulting things about God
cathedral	large church where a bishop is based
census	count of the population
charismatic	moved by the power of the Holy Spirit to praise God aloud
Christ	title given to Jesus by Christians that means "Messiah"
clergy	specially trained Christians who are priests, pastors, or ministers
confirmation	ceremony at which someone affirms his or her baptism
congregation	group of people at a church service or who attend a specific church
creed	statement of belief
cremate	burn a dead body
crucifixion	act of killing someone by nailing him or her to a cross
denomination	branch of Protestantism
disciple	someone who followed Jesus while he was still alive
Epiphany	day on which three wise men reached the stable where Jesus was born
eternal	lasting forever
Eucharist	"thanksgiving"—another name for the service of Holy Communion
Evangelical	organized around the principle that all people can be saved from sin through God's gift of forgiveness
fast	go without food and drink for religious reasons
font	container of water used in baptism
grace	gift of forgiveness, freely given; also a prayer before or after meals
Hebrew	traditional language of the Jews
Holy Communion	time during Christian worship service when people take bread and wine to remember Jesus; also called Eucharist
icon	religious painting of Jesus, the Virgin Mary, or a saint

iconostasis	screen that divides an Orthodox church
incense	spice with a strong smell burned as part of worship
Jew	follower of the religion of Judaism
Lent	solemn church season leading up to Easter
Liturgy	service of Holy Communion in Orthodox churches; also another name for worship
Messiah	one chosen or anointed by God
missionary	person who travels to teach other people about his or her religion
monk	man who has dedicated his life to God
Nativity	Jesus' birth
nun	woman who has dedicated her life to God
Orthodox	"right belief"—a branch of Christianity
patriarch	leader of the Orthodox Church
Pentecost	festival at which the early Christians received the Holy Spirit
Pentecostal	group of Christians who emphasize individual experiences and recognize special gifts, such as faith healing
pilgrim	someone who makes a journey for religious reasons
pilgrimage	journey made for religious reasons
pope	leader of the Roman Catholic Church; Bishop of Rome
priest	member of the clergy or leader of a group of worshipers
prophet	someone who gives people messages that have been sent by God
Protestant	Christian who believes that people are saved by faith and not by doing good deeds
pulpit	raised platform in a church used for preaching or reading God's word
resurrection	being raised from the dead; coming back to life
Roman Catholic	branch of Christianity whose members believe that the pope is God's earthly authority
saint	any baptized believer in Christ, or someone now dead whom people consider to have been close to God
shrine	holy place; often where a saint is buried
sin	wrongdoing that separates a person from God
Temple	building in which followers of the Jewish religion hold services
theology	system or theory of religious belief
total immersion	baptism in which a person's entire body is placed underwater
Trinity	belief that God is three persons in one: Father, Son, and Holy Spirit
vision	dreamlike religious experience
vow	solemn promise a person makes that commits him or her to a certain path in life
wise man	one of three ancient Middle Eastern rulers who were said to have brought gifts to the infant Jesus shortly after his birth

Further Information

Bahr, Ann Marie B. *Christianity*. Philadelphia: Chelsea House, 2004.

Brown, Alan. *The Bible and Christianity*. North Mankato, Minn.: Smart Apple Media, 2004.

Brown, Stephen F., and Khaled Anatolios. *Catholicism and Orthodox Christianity*. New York: Facts on File, 2006.

Ganeri, Anita. *Christian Festivals Throughout the Year*. North Mankato, Minn.: Smart Apple Media, 2003.

Teece, Geoff. *Christianity*. North Mankato, Minn.: Smart Apple Media, 2005.

Index